Worth More Growing

01 02 03 04 05 26 25 24 23 22

Caitlin Press Inc.
3375 Ponderosa Way
Qualicum Beach, BC V9K 2J8
www.caitlin-press.com

Text and cover design by Vici Johnstone
Cover image: Istock 1183575116
Edited by Christine Lowther
Printed in Canada

Caitlin Press Inc. acknowledges financial support from the Government of Canada and the Canada Council for the Arts, and the Province of British Columbia through the British Columbia Arts Council and the Book Publisher's Tax Credit.

Library and Archives Canada Cataloguing in Publication

Worth more growing : youth poets pay homage to trees / edited by Christine Lowther.

Lowther, Christine, 1967- editor.
Canadiana 20220222991 | ISBN 9781773860978 (softcover)

LCSH: Trees—Poetry. | CSH: School verse, Canadian (English) | CSH: Canadian poetry
   (English)—21st century. | LCGFT: Poetry.

LCC PS8287.T74 W67 2022 | DDC C811.008/0364216—dc23

Worth More Growing

Youth Poets Pay Homage to Trees

Edited by Christine Lowther

Caitlin Press 2022

"Trees are dolphins and mothers, trees are best friends and providers, trees are medicine and wisdom ... in this joyous book young writers share with us their relations with trees. Experience the wonder of growing up to trees: from a seven-year-old thanking a tree for unicorn cake all the way to high school students trembling at the endangerment of forests. Earthtastic!!"

—Sonnet L'Abbe, author of *Sonnet's Shakespeare*

"What a joy it was reading the tree poems in this collection. From the unabashed innocence of the early grades' love of nature to the heartbreak and awareness of the older students recognizing the damage of climate change, these poems run the gamut of experience."

—RC Weslowski, Canadian Individual Poetry Slam Champion, 2 time World Cup of Poetry Slam Finalist and author of "My Soft Response to the Wars" on Write Bloody North Press

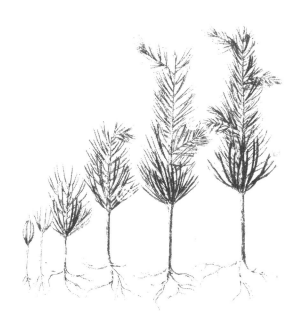

CONTENTS

GRADE FOUR

GRADE FIVE

GRADE EIGHT

KINDERGARTEN

Animals In Trees

—Chevy Trakarnsilpa

Animals in trees
Jumpy Red Squirrels
Animals in trees
Sleepy Brown Koalas
Animals in trees,
Chirping Blue Birds
Animals in trees
Hungry Giant Pandas
Animals in trees
Camouflaging Chameleons

GRADE ONE

My Maple

—*Alisa Wanyan*

My favourite tree is a maple tree
I met my tree a long time ago
I love the colours of the tree in fall
      They are orange, green, red, and gold.

Dear Trees

—Angela Wang

Dear Apple Tree,
I love to pick apples from your lovely tree.
Your apples are shiny, bright, and sweet.
They look like red coats in the summer.

Dear Cherry Tree,
You are very beautiful in spring
With your pink blossoms and petals
And you make me very very happy.

Dear Unicorn Tree,
You are very beautiful and talented
because you can dance
and I love your gold horns.
And thank you for giving unicorn cake
from your silver leaves.
You are awesome.

Love,
  Angela

My Fiddle Tree

—Harcus Yang

A fiddle tree is a whale shaped tree
and you will need some tips to find the fiddle tree.
The tips are you need to find scrambled leaves
and a scrambled tree.

The leaves will lead you to the way
and you will finally find
the fiddle tree.

My Tree

—Saifeier Zhang

The tree in my garden
It is special because it was planted
last year

And it is a pine tree
It smells like grapevine

It is bigger than me
It is too big to hug

I love it because it is from last Christmas
This tree reminds of Christmas
It's my hiding spot.

Warren's Tree

—Warren Liu

My first favourite tree is
in the park and I can climb it.
It stays alive for four seasons,
even winter.
I put tools up there
just like my treehouse.

My second favourite tree
is in my backyard.
I found it today.
I knew it was the one that I love
because it has beautiful leaves.
I like the shape of the leaves.
They are shaped like a boat.
The tree is taller than my dad.

GRADE TWO

Me and My Maple Tree

—Doris Zhu

I have a maple tree
in the backyard

It has beautiful red leaves
and singing birds

There are blue jays, robins,
and hummingbirds.

Once Irene and I dug
for worms and fed birds

I like the tree because it
gives me sap

And I can make Canada flags
out of its maple leaves.

Pine Tree I See Through My Window

—Lanice Chen

The tree is larger than a person.
The tree is spiky because it is a pine tree.
It's still green in the wintertime.
I can't hold the tree by myself because I am so tiny.
If the tree looks at me it will think I am an ant.
It is thinking of growing taller than my house.
It does not want to get chopped down.

GRADE THREE

Triple Trunk

—Angelina Xu

I found a tree in a park
It is not an evergreen tree
I call it triple trunk tree
It is a very tall tree
It has heart shaped leaves
   as big as my palms
It has vertical grooves
It has a seat
where the trunks meet
I choose this tree because
   I could sit there
And I could read there
It gave me shade
And I gave it water.

My Favourite Trees

—Luciana Lu

My favourite trees look a lot like
skeleton hands in winter

I am pretty sure they are birch trees
They look really neat in a row

They are reaching for the sky
with lots of branches I can climb

I wonder if I climbed one
Would I touch a cloud?

If I were a tree...

—Luciana Lu

If I were a tree I would be strong and sturdy
so animals could rest on me.
Then I would never be alone.

In the winter
squirrels will make a nest in my trunk
And be snug and cozy.

In the spring
I will be full of rolly pollies
Which isn't the most pleasant thing.

In the fall
there would be mice and owls
Chasing each other.

In the summer
my branches would be filled with colourful birds
Singing their songs.

I would have branches that reach for the sky
so children can climb on them.

If only I were a tree…

GRADE FOUR

The Little Tree

—Holly Zhang

There was once a big pine tree
in the big forest

Its bark was as smooth as you.
It did not have any branches,
and it never grew.

There was a big hole in it
that always got bigger.

And in the big hole
there was a small little tree
that grew and grew and grew.

One day it got so big that
the big tree in the big forest
disappeared.

The Cedar Tree

—Isabel Wang

If I were a cedar tree
I would have clean green leaves

If I were a cedar tree
I would have a perfectly round hole
with food for a squirrel.

If I were a cedar tree in spring
I would have a cozy nest
in my branches for the birds

If I were a cedar tree in winter
I would be a cozy place for animals to sleep

If I were a cedar tree
I could be a canoe for those
who don't know how to drive

If I were a cedar tree
I could be paper for you
to write poems on me.

Mirror Tree

—Matthew Ng

My friend and I used to fly airplanes under our tree

They always got stuck
it was fun getting the paper planes out of the tree

The tree fell down after a really strong wind
Small branches grow on the stump that is left

Maybe the tree will become big again.

Small branches grow on the stump that is left
The tree fell down after a really strong wind

it was fun getting the paper planes out of the tree
They always got stuck

My friend and I used to fly airplanes under our tree.

Untitled verses

—Rio Green

Starting a seed
Looking like a weed
I start to proceed
Into a tree
I am moving, magic and wise
and my long tangly branches reach to the sky

----

still morning, birds singing, we sway
afternoon sun brings a twitch of wind
tickling our branches
night light by stars and moon
here we watch
all are life

Earthtastic

(an acrostic poem)

—*Rio Green*

Wild
Elegant
Special and strong
Tall
Evergreen
Resilient
Nature

Red
Exciting
Daring

Caring
Eccentric
Delightful
Artistic
Rustic

Treasure
Roots
Extra beautiful
Earthtastic

Western Red Cedar

—Rio Green

my roots deep in the ground
swirling and winding their way around
steadying me at all times
storm, rain, lightning, thunder
my trunk growing high trying hard to reach the sky of blue
my branches steady me too, giving me food from the bright green colour of
my braided leaves
I am alive
I feel what you do, I can see you, I can hear you
we are the same

Take care of me.

Dreams

—Rio Green

Ever since I was a seedling
I dreamed of growing up tall enough to see the beautiful sights of nature
the big trees surrounding me
the mossy ground, spongy bogs, muddy sound
but when I grew up I had a view of a never-ending clearcut
no birds sang, no animals came
I was alone
in time a few shrubs of Salal grew, just a bit of company, but that was all

the earth is asking us to help
Act now
we need to stand up for what keeps us alive

My Apple Tree

—Ryan Kossari

My apple tree has great height,
It also has some might.

Although my tree is standing straight,
When I look at it I lose my hate.

I feel my tree is watching,
morning, noon, and evening.

I like to talk to my tree,
because it makes me feel free.

My Maple Tree

—Ryan Kossari

I have a maple tree in my school,
I know my tree is not a fool.

I watch it as the days go past,
As it says hello to me and the grass.

Every day it grows a bit,
So I like to watch it.

Whenever I get close to my tree,
My heart feels more lovely.

A Tree Song

—*Soleil Zhang*

Trees swish swish blocking my way
to a meadow full of their flower friends
Trying to protect them.

I touch the bark of one tree
The heart beat coursing through the roots.

I sit down listening to a soft lovely melody.
La la thump swishhh,
La la thump swishhhh

The sound so powerful
I start to write my own song called
In the meadow

This is the inspiration I have been longing for
I spend time with my tree friends
While the flowers fly into the setting sky.

I love trees in a different way than people.

GRADE FIVE

Trees

—*Alyssa Liu*

Under them we seek
Shade on a hot summer day
With a picnic and friends
In the month of May.

Their leaves can be green
And other colours too!
Orange, red, brown
Just for you.

Please let them stay here on earth.
Keep them alive.
Let them thrive
And they'll keep us alive.

Bristlecone Pine

—Alyssa Liu

If I could be any tree I wanted
I'd be a Bristlecone Pine
They live for a long time.

I want to live as a tree
because I want to see what changes
In the landscape
or how much global warming
will affect the Earth.

The oldest Bristlecone Pine
is over 5,000 years of age,

Can you imagine?
The world's oldest clonal tree is:
Old Tjikko, a 9,550-year-old Norway spruce
in the Fulufjället Mountains in Sweden.

I want to be a tree to protect people
from the big summer sun.

Weeping Willow

—Annie Shen

Leaves are scattered around me
The willow tree branches hang over me

They are sturdy
And when I pull back on the branches

I kick off from the trunk
I feel the wind brush my face
I take a breath.

The willow and I find peace.

Trees

—Anthony Li

Every summer a tree adds a coat
The more coats the wiser
but with one swing of an axe
all that wisdom wasted
by the lumberjack

Once beautiful air
dark clouds bloom
choke animals
now barren land

Lush green forests
stripped for our wants
before full of life
now deserted

This Story Stumped Me

—Anthony Li

A little stump
holding up lives of green
holding up the age of time

It tells stories

if you have patience
to listen
and to wait by the roots

The Tree Calls

—Bronwyn Moes

I hear my name
Call from the forest night
As it calls,
My skin goes soft
My legs go numb
My body shivers
It was a dream I thought
I wake up in the forest
I hear my name
Wondering
I see a big, tall, beautiful tree
I put my ear next to the tree
I hear a buzzing sound from bees and bugs
Leaves swing in the powerful wind
I see sap
Dripping from high spots
Sap drips on my hands
I feel it
It feels smooth and lovely
I take my time looking at it
I hear the voice from
All the trees
I see their leaves swinging
The sap dripping
The branches swaying
I see everything
I hear the voice from all the trees
I see their branches swaying in
The wind
I see everything
How all the trees feel
I take my time to sit next to every tree
I feel their fears
I sit next to the trees in peace and quiet
To listen

The Fallen Tree

—Charley McLean

There it is lying down,
Watching the axe man who felled it.
Tears running down its face,
It takes a moment to appreciate
The blue bird who goes by every day,
The wind, who says "hey."
Then it realizes where the wind is going,
To the place where it will soon be.
To the place where they all go, sooner or later.
It is the place that they go when they are done,
And as it takes its last breath and says,
"I am now one… one with the sun."

Trees, Trees, Trees

—Chester Trakarnsilpa

Trees so beautiful,
It feels like velvet
Trees so beautiful,
It tastes like mint
Trees so beautiful,
It sounds like eagles calling
Trees so beautiful,
It smells like vanilla
Trees so beautiful,
It looks like the colour of nature

Trees

—Emily Qian

Trees are all long trunks and branches
They are monuments
Filled with the wisdom of the past

Every single leaf is a sign of determination
Every single branch tells you to have hope

Trees' hearts are like human hearts
They are our best friends
When we are lonely
And devastated

They are with us
No matter what
They are like parents

They cuddle you when you are sad
They kiss you when you are scared
They remind you when you forget

Our air providers
Without them we wouldn't be able to thrive
They are our rescuers

The first ones couldn't live
The world would be nothing
We would live in a dark hole

There are people trying to cut them down
Even with all the things a tree can do
Even with all the things a tree can do…

The Big Floppy Monster

—Emily Qian

It was a big, floppy overgrown
Monster
It looked too old to be in this world
Yet connected to me by an invisible silver thread
I sat down beneath it

Its branches hang down
With wisdom until the top of its fingers
And the end of its toenails
It has been here before we arrived
And will be here when we fall

Its leaves are still shining
Like a magnificent bird
on its travels

Its big trunk is a symbol
for what people have gone through
It notes our worries
And celebrates our accomplishments

It smells green and young
As can be
Its touch is scaly and old
It is wise as can be
But its heart remains as young
As ever

The smell
Reminds me of home
Of the great grass
And beautiful flowers
And of wise trees and floating clouds
Oh, it reminds me of nature
The scaly touch
Was not scary

It was a touch I
Always wanted to have
I have a connection with it
For we both
Love nature

Nobody has realized its
Special feeling
The leader of the trees
Old, but young
That is standing there
In the troubles and happiest
Of times

Dolphin Tree

—Emily Qian

The tree is a dolphin!
Energetic as it sways,
Just like a group of playful dolphins.

It hollers as it sways towards the music
Of nature
Just like dolphins squeaking underwater.

Its branches twirl
Just like a dolphin's fin twirling in delight.

It watches the world with careful eyes
Like a dolphin when hunting for food.

From bottom to top it changes colours
Thanks to the sun
From bottom to top dolphins change colours
Thanks to the mysterious underground shadows.

Brightly every morning, the trees dance to the wind
Energetically every morning the dolphins jump
with the current of the sea

Filled with wisdom, the tree begins its day
Its smart mind—a playful dolphin.

The Twisted Tree

—*Ethan Wang*

There is this tree near my home
that I can't seem to climb.
It looks very easy but
when I try
it's impossible.

I can't walk around it
it is near a pond.

It hides a lot of things,
it is so leafy but
it is the leafy plants surrounding it
that get all the credit.

One thing we have in common is
we get on people's nerves.

There is almost no way to get on top of us
(unless they've already been there from the start).

I bet I challenge some people
the way this tree challenges me.

I just can't seem to figure out
how to climb it.

Tree Fun

—Lucas Yu

There is a tree at my school that I really like.
When I'm allowed to work outside
I sit on my tree.
It's fun to be high up,
it's comfortable.
The tree is easy to climb,
It has lots of strong branches,
it isn't too tall.
I can climb on it hoping that no one spots me
when we play manhunt, at recess
The tree is still there and I love it
when we play manhunt at recess.
I can climb on it hoping that no one spots me.
it isn't too tall.
It has lots of strong branches.
The tree is easy to climb,
it's comfortable.
It's fun to be high up,
I sit on my tree,
When I'm allowed to work outside
There is a tree at my school that I really like.

A blossom

—Saioa Ouyoumjian

A cherry blossom pink or white?
My flowers bloom, soft and delicate.
My blossoms are beautiful, but make the most for they only have two
weeks to live.

600 different kinds of me, can you tell the difference?
I signify love but have two weeks to live, do you know why?

Many people come to see me and my family.
We are a sight to see: pink, white, and yellow blossoms on the ground and
on our branches.
Take one, keep it safe, a reminder of beauty.

WAIT! Before you leave, understand my ways, my reasons.
Look over my words—what do you find? Look carefully.
Make the most, 600 different kinds, a reminder of beauty, get it yet?

I am a cherry blossom: short life, pretty, and generic to many.
But I am me and you are you and if you don't act you might miss it.
My final question: do you see the cherry blossom in you?

Sakuras [Japanese for Cherry Blossoms]

—Samantha Pon

Cherry blossoms, delicate and small,
Something you don't grow in the mall
On the other side of Earth, a country celebrates high
A festival in honour of these flowers, Sakuras, floating in the sky
Softly, gently, all around, they fall, grow, then rise

People ponder, "Just how beautiful are they?"
And enjoy their beauty each day
Mother Nature provides us surprises, which include
Cherry blossoms

Springtime, these rosy and fragrant flowers dance around
"Most beautiful flowers!" they should be crowned
I stare in awe of this mystery,
How Mother Earth has created these throughout history,
Cherry blossoms

A Tree Outside

—Ryder Hsu

He is the protector of our house
the tree in my backyard
from the time the house was built
now more than twice its height
with moss around
he reaches to the heavens

The line of sap
along the side of the tree
like a waterfall
gives my family luck
happiness, and peace

The bumpy bark
gives it a pattern unique
from other trees

Although I am short
and he is tall
we both are the happy ones
in our family

He is so ancient
and has formed a hill
for himself

I love him
and he loves me
his roots are spread so wide
he has a very firm grip on the ground
I also have a very firm grip on the ground

Forever, Evergreen: Spruce

—*Ryder Hsu*

Shy Bark
Their brown wood
Green leaves
And edible buds

Their cones,
And leaves
Survive all year round
Forever, Evergreen.

Spruce Trees
Tall standing,
Of two hundred feet
And large branches

Spruce are old
Never chop any Spruce down
Let them grow, instead for 250 years
Make it 1000, it's definitely possible

But never get them
Confused with Fir
'Cause both of them
Deserve lots of respect

They give you air,
They give you joy
They give you amazement

Without Spruce
Without you

Forever, Evergreen
They stand tall
Forever, Evergreen
They give you life

Trees are Masters

—Ryder Hsu

Trees are masters
I don't believe
Green will never fill up the world
Soon greenness will return to 1 million years ago
But it is false to think
Climate change is nothing
We must change our habits
I do not think
Trees are ugly,
Trees in the ground are useless.
If you like opposition, then
Trees are of no use, and
The opposite fills my head.
I regret it when
We keep doing what we are doing,
I say to the trees.

(read now from the bottom up)

In the Middle of the Park

—Ryder Hsu

If I were a tree, I would be an apple tree
I would happily sit there
And look at children play
In the park

If I were a tree, I would give children apples
And let them climb up and down
my branches and trunk
I would be in the middle of the park

When I was sad
I would rain leaves
When I was happy
I'd grow

When it was raining
I'd grow
When it was sunny
I'd grow

Raining days would be my favourite
Sunny days next
Snowy days wouldn't
I would be cold and bare

If I were a tree
I would provide oxygen
And help the environment
I would be the tree
Who would never be chopped down

If I were a tree
I would be the tree of the park
And children would love me

I would be the happiest tree

Dancer

—Ty Joudrey

An arbutus tree
clings to the cliff, a dancer
Arms stretch to the sun

GRADE SIX

Native Mother

—Jon Manson

Native mother
collects healing tea leaves
deep in the forest.

This year I planted a tree

—Krishti Khandelwal

This year I planted a tree.
I pottered 'round the garden, and I felt free!
'The cute little seedling will grow up.'
That thought ran in my head, while I was hit with a gentle breeze.

I looked at the rest of the garden,
With unique flowers all around.
Many petals and seeds with a marvellous colour,
While that beautiful, unique masterpiece grew from the ground.

And I felt happy!
That plant's sprouts were cute indeed.
It made me feel so calm,
the leaves, the flowers, and the sprouting seeds.

The air was so fresh,
It was cold enough perfectly.
And I looked at my tree,
As I thought what it would be.

How it can help us,
How long it would last,
How it made me feel better,
How in the future, I'll think about the past.

I'll look back in my memories,
While I'll sit beneath that calming tree.

Save Us

—Ocea Green

Before you cut me down
let me tell you a little story
a little story about me

The moon casts shadows across my trunk
tree frogs cling to my bark
singing the world to sleep
then rest their heads on mossy logs

All is still and calm

Morning mist hangs in the air
robin red breast sings the world awake
he calls me home, along with all of the
animals who burrow in my trunk
the birds who nest in my branches
the plants whose roots use mine as a shelter
the mosses who creep up my trunk
and weave their way around my branches
the fungi whose roots rest on my roots

And you
I clean your air and help you breathe
I am a living home for you
and everything surrounding me

Save me

I am a Tree

—*Ocea Green*

I am a tree
I can feel hurt and pain
I can see our world crumbling
I can hear of your thoughtless actions
but I also see kindness and care just not yet sparked.
Everyone is too distracted in this new world of money and technologies;
many have forgotten what really keeps them alive, the earth.
You need to act NOW.
Because what you do to us trees you do to yourselves.

I Am a Tree

—Paul Phillos

I am a tree and woe is me.
I am to be cut
And I have no rebut.

I wish I was curvy
Or that my wood was white
For I am to become furniture tonight.

Tomorrow I will be on a cart
The dirt and my roots
So far apart.

I wonder if I will become
A chair or a couch
Maybe a shelf… ouch!

I stand tall.
Survive windstorms and fires.
Have yet to fall.

Let's not forget
The people who visit here
They get caught in my leafy net.

My last wish is that
I don't become firewood
'cause for a tree, that is very *not* good.

The Cycle of Life

—Tanis Cortens

The
acorn fell
from the great
oak onto the squirrel's
head. The squirrel picked up
the nut and hid it in a hole. When
winter came, the squirrel snuggled
up in its burrow under the oak and
slept while a mighty storm
blew up. Snow came down from
the clouds and covered everything
in a white blanket. The wind
howled around the oak,
shaking it back and forth
like a reed in the breeze. After
many hours of resisting, the ancient
oak fell with a crash, taking several
other trees with it. The next
morning, an early spring rain refreshed
the land, bringing with it the promise
of new life. The buried acorn
began to sprout, slowly but surely
becoming taller. Years later,
that same sprout was as tall
and strong as the oak before
had been. An acorn fell from that
great oak onto a squirrel's head.
The squirrel looked at the nut
and smiled. The cycle of
life
had
begun
again.

GRADE SEVEN

A Tree is Life

—Aidan Zhang

A tree is life around us
the air we breathe
the branches we climb.

When I look out my window
I see eight trees;
there is one that I love.

Planted by my grandfather
the tree stands in our yard
taller than any of the other trees

I smell dirt and fresh air
when I stand beneath it.

I feel a sense of *Littleness*
when I stand beside it.

I don't know if the tree loves me
I hope it knows that
I love it.

Stumped

—Angelina Sunwoo

The fir tree down the block, was chopped by
people much younger than it.

One year it was there, the next it was gone.
I moved away for bit, that's all it took
To cut away an ancient being.

It was a tall, towering, friendly tree
That protected me from rain.
As tall as the cable poles beside it.
I was too short to climb it, but
I liked to play in the branches
Trying to hide from my mom.

I loved the tree,
it made the grounds look whole.
Then I moved away.
Now—a stump, moss-covered,
and widely ignored.

Today, a lost dog sign is pinned to
the bark. The tree is lost too.
The stump is worn and slightly torn,
nearly as tall as me,
Its bark—thick, and delicately layered
like fungus—peeling.

Impressive looking still, even if they
cut it very roughly.

If I Were a Tree

—Angelina Sunwoo

If I were a tree, I would welcome
the little and big birds into my arms.
I'd brush gently against the heads of passers by.
I'd block trails.

If I were a maple tree, I would produce
as much sap as possible so humans can
spend a comfortable winter.

I'd listen to animals chitter-chatter
speak to tree friends through
the wood wide web.

I'd give owls and rabbits hiding places and homes.
To only talk to trees wouldn't be lonely at all.

If I were a tree, I'd dance with the wind:
sometimes fierce and whipping,
sometimes slow and dreamy,
but always rooted to the ground.

I'd dance with the forest
to the birds singing on our arms
and the river rushing by.

I'd help younger trees grow steady
take advice from older trees;
they have discovered tricks younger trees don't think of.
I would want to become a wise old tree.

I would tell the humans: "Do not cut
any more of us! Don't build buildings
in our place.
We are irreplaceable."

Birch

—*Carter Witter*

There is a birch where bluebirds like to perch.
They saw a grey squirrel that made them lurch.

The Mystery Tree

—Jet Robertson

I don't know what species of tree this is, but I know it's nice.
It looks like the bottom of the white scratched bark has been captured by
yellow fungi.
The rest is spotted with moss and lichen, light and dark greens.
One part of the tree has been chopped somehow, which means now it can
show off its chipped bright wood grain, swirling endlessly.
However, some is rotting with holes in the green tinted wood.
There are little branches poking off but not overtaking the strong tall trunk.
And when you follow the tree into the ground, the roots begin spreading
through the soft squishy dirt, soon to disappear out of sight.

Old Growth

—Malia Ashby

I am here, you are here.
You cannot see me,
but I see you.

You are much older than me,
much wiser than me,
much stronger than me.

In a way you have created growth,
created a space for those growing.

You do not live in your original form,
but you are here.

The space I sit now holds your ashes,
You once lived here,
You are still here,
You make here.

There didn't used to be fields of berries,
lined in rows,
restricted from growing
wherever they chose.

There used to be you.
Growing jagged and tall,
filling yourself with rings for all.
You would reach for the clouds and
dig through the grounds,
surrounded by those who guided your way.

I sit upon you now,
resting.

So, you don't see me,
but I see you.

The tree for me

—Noelle Fung

The Aspen trees, BC is where they grow
Looking like one big oreo
They can be shaved into bedding
And hamsters will have fun running,
Digging, stuffing, and rolling. Whoa!
When Autumn is here, the leaves glow
A beautiful glow in yellow
All will say, Aspen is stunning

Leaves descend as winter follows
Half bare, fully bare, all leaves go
Snowflakes falling with hints of bling
Snow landing softly and will cling
A staggering landscape, we know

The Colours of Maple Trees

—*Riley Tam*

The spring is red like apples.
Summer is green like lettuce.
Fall is orange and yellow like candy corn.
But winter has none except branches.

Summer is green like lettuce.
And frogs and kiwis.
But winter has none except branches.
Yet, snow falls making the branches like cotton and clouds.

And dinosaurs and kiwis.
And polar bears and feathers.
And tigers and rubber ducks.
And Canada and strawberries.

And polar bears and feathers.
Fall is orange and yellow like candy corn.
And Canada and strawberries.
The spring is red like apples.

Fir Tree

—Roselyn Tam

All you can hear
Is a solemn silence

A peaceful fir tree
Atop the rolling hills
Of Queen Elizabeth Park

As you step closer
The deep, lush green needles
Reach out to you
Bristly
But not sharp

It stands strong
Scrapes the sky

The branches start abundant
At the base
Transform into a
Pointy top

If I were a tree

—Roselyn Tam

If I were a tree
I'd live in a forest
Surrounded by
Plenty of other trees

I'd wish my trunk
Had rings like Saturn

And had roots
That cascade
Down the forest floor

I'd wish my branches
Were as long
As a flowing river

To hold many birds on my
Outstretched arms

I'd want the sunlight
To stream down
My woody trunk

And radiate
On my luscious
Green leaves

I'd want to live
Secluded
From humans

Because I can't
Run from
Saws or flames

Birch

—*Sofia Varma-Vitug*

This birch tree branches out into three trunks,
like my different interests,
finding new paths to grow into the world

I sit on the stump at its base
and braid the branches as if they were my sister's hair

This stump is like the parts of my life
that I've left behind

At the bottom, the trunk is brown
unlike the rest of the tree, which is white
It shows how I've grown through a new chapter
of my life

With patches that look like
arrows pointing up into the crown,
a fountain of thoughts

They fall back and wave in the wind
like my long hair

The tree stands confident
like I have to stand through covid
and the rest of high school

Replaced

—Sofia Varma-Vitug

There was a tree
at Minoru track.
And during track meets,
I would climb it.

I climbed up, trying not to rip my track clothes.
And there I would sit,
watching the races and the long jump,
climbing down when it was my turn.

But one day,
they were pouring concrete
in the space where my tree had stood
there was no more grass to sit on
—no more tree.

Now a swimming pool is there.

I had to find a different tree.
This one is near the finish line.
Climbing this tree is like being in a different world,
it's like a little cave hideout.
I like to sit and spy on people from high up in the branches.
This tree is fun,
but I also miss the other one.

I hope this tree stays standing.

Still Standing

—Sofia Varma-Vitug

Trees are like ghosts that can't move
they watch over the place they live

but they can't stop people from
harming them

they can't speak out
but they communicate with us
By
Wilting
Blooming
Growing
Falling
Changing colours
Letting go of leaves

Trees that blossom
before their leaves
are special

like cherry-blossom trees
they invite me to climb

Cherry trees are a
a perfect height
with sturdy branches

The trunk is tough,
the flowers are so delicate.

GRADE EIGHT

As Wind Blows Through Willow

—Aisha Hsu

Alone on the waterside
gazing at the coastline,
observing with eyes of gold,
silently.

Waving her ribbons
in the dance,
responding to the sea, as
seagulls call out irregular

rhythms.
Like her hair.
Like the green lines on
the water's reflection.

Like the waves lapping
the rocky shores.
Her whispers on a bright day, carrying
across the ocean.

Her silent wails on a stormy night,
seeing sailors
crash onto shore, looking
desperate and bedraggled.

She lends them shelter
and stands, unmoving—
watching them with sightless eyes,
touching them with leafy fingers.

Murmuring her stories
gesturing her arms,
perhaps in greeting—
as wind blows through willow.

Oak Tree

—Kevin Wang

Oh you beautiful living creature in the distance!
Curved into the shape of a heart
How can I ever forget you?

My eyes shine as they look upon you
My heart brightens to see your beautiful leaves sway
Like an ocean wave.

Oak tree
You stand tall on the hill—
the greatest creation of mother earth!

Embody all beauty in nature
Fill the air with your scent
If only I could live with you

And you live with me
forever.

Lessons of Trees

—Kristina Bedford

Like a leaf I have fallen,
I have fallen into despair.
Streams of pain and loneliness fall from my eyelids.
I thought I could erase it, forget it, hide it.
Get rid of it somehow,
But the pain and remembrance would not leave me until someone understood.
No one did.
But something did understand.

When I was left alone,
Deserted in the woods.
When I was forgotten by society.
I was left with the trees.

You never know true comfort unless the strong branches wrap around you.
You will never feel blessed,
Until like them you are rooted to the ground.
They were the only beings that understood.
The ones that didn't question my looks, personality, or beliefs.
The ones that saved me,
The trees.

I recall words from my mother and they encircle my mind in a vortex of remembrance.
"Hold on to the trees, because they can understand."

Once, in the bitter past, that sentence seemed confusing.
Words that did not form a correct sentence.
Her words make sense now.
Death may be bitter but they have witnessed centuries of it.
Isolation targets me but also to the one lonely willow on the top of the mountain.
Arrows pierce their bark but the trees still stand.
They have experienced the pain and horrors that society brings the world.
And now they teach me.

Words that once hurt me,
Started to brush off my shoulder.
I realized a name only lives if it defines you.
Their names didn't define me.
I am now like the trees.
Society cannot destroy me.
So long as I am rooted to the ground.

HU *(from the Mandarin Chinese word meaning both "to protect" and "to breathe")*

—Lucy Yang's Grade 8 English class at Burnsview Secondary School, 2018-19

Two Tree Poems

—Oafe Cheung

Early one morning,
a Sunday afternoon,
the trees began to whistle
while flowers bloomed,
and across the street,
a girl could see
a whirling chainsaw
cutting a tree.
She watched in horror
as the tree fell,
the sound as clear
as a chiming bell.
Tears dripped down
from the girl's eyes;
this horrid event
was quite a surprise.
This small little tree
had been like a friend,
someone who stayed
until the end.
Through the window
the girl would peer,
the little tree
seeming so near.
Now she watched
and the men worked,
at the window
she continued to lurk.
As the truck started up
and drove away,
the girl was left
on a horrid day.

Looking out the window
One can see many things
The birds chirping
And leaves swaying in the wind
All beautiful scenes and sounds
That make up a humble view
But all good things must come to an end
Trees can be many things
Since they can provide so much
And trees can be friends
For they stand longer than man
And have seen much more than we
But diseases and age can cause all that
To rot away and die
Objects with sentimental value
Are always the hardest to let go
No matter how small
Or how valuable
And the worse way to lose something
Is when it dies.

GRADE NINE

Night Time in a Forest

—Sylvester Gross-Hamburger

At night the trees are still and barely shake
And when they do leave sawdust in their wake
Their sacral bones score slipstreams underground
Neuronic storks soaring without a sound
And deep below if caves were hollowed out
And if we were to follow down that route
We'd see the roots go curling 'cross the wall
Like ancient humans fingerpainted scrawl
Or carvings chipped in stone or on a mast
The forest sings the song of ages past
For why should only mushrooms be conjoined
And why should only trees be so eloigned
The green skinned beast lies in her verdant bed
With diamond moss a crown upon her head
Her fingers float like time lapse satellites
They sit and watch the operas of night
Her radios a station of white noise
And wind the only singer she employs
Be still at night and you can hear her breathe
A sound of bird calls filtered through a sieve
The water cycle pulls her rising breast
And worlds may even move at her behest

GRADE ELEVEN

Trees/seerT

—Bowen Wang

The old tree withers away
The soil wastes away
more insect than soil now
as if the insects are weeping
they migrate to a new home
like Immigrants fleeing from a civil war
From the mountains
From the kelp forests
parallel worlds
with their long vines and fast growth
the trees expand into the sky
Even the trees in your backyard are mourned by nature
eventually all that's left is a gravestone
This tree stump once marked a mighty tree.

Eventually all that's left is a gravestone
Even the trees in your backyard are mourned by nature
the trees expand into the sky
with their long vines and fast growth
parallel worlds
From the kelp forests
From the mountains
like Immigrants fleeing from a civil war
they migrate to a new home
as if the insects are weeping
more insect than soil now
The soil wastes away
The old tree withers away

Sitka Spruce and Stories Told

—Maya Mior

I spend time in the woods, when I can.
I've learned that of all the world, trees are the least likely to tell secrets,
so when I am exhausted by sirens and shouts, I find myself at the trunks.

I've learned that if you spend enough time with one tree, if you learn the
feel of the twigs underfoot,
you can sometimes hear it talk back.
That if you bare your soul, feel deeply, and whisper, you might hear a sym-
pathetic sigh rustle the leaves.

My soul has been closed off for far too long,
so I find a tree, lean on the trunk,
and speak.
Tell the first story that comes to mind, words rambling and wrapping the
branches.
I hear no response, but have more stories to tell.

I return the next day,
tell all I can think of, let my voice catch on the needles and cones.
Unwrap the bandages
covering my spirit, show the wounds
without shame.

Finally, I hear a simple chuckle.
At the simple trials of my moments on this earth,
the tree laughs a quiet reminder of the triviality of it all.

So I return again,
and sit at the base of the trunk for hours, listening.
Hear the centuries of stories it has to tell.

I listen as the tree tells me about moments.
Teaches of how each moment contains within it a thousand lifetimes.

The mayfly, it tells me, lives no more than 24 hours.
1440 minutes of life, passion, and death,
the only goal to reproduce. To stave off the vast expanse by bringing new life.
 I have lived 6094 lifetimes.
Calculator in hand, I learn that the tree has lived 1,825,000 lifetimes.

Unfathomable to me, but to the universe
nothing more than a moment.

I begin to spend my lifetimes carefully,
climbing branches,
weaving between trunks,
listening for lessons that stumble from twig to twig.

Sometimes we speak, but mostly we are silent;
the roots teach me to soak up lessons from beneath the surface;
still-green needles blanket the soft earth, show the value found in detritus.

Moments (lifetimes) end, eventually. The timer runs out, the final curtain
call.
I return the next week,
see wooden shreds, the remnants of branches.
Scattered seeds call to mind the mayfly—this artificial plain will not be
permanent.
Sit in the clearcut expanse, and hear no whispers.

So I tell another story.

GRADE TWELVE

I Swear I Saw their Boughs Tremble

—Cedar Forest

I swear I saw their boughs tremble
I swear I saw their leaves shiver
I swear I felt the intake of breath
as the evening sun struck their bark
I felt them rejoice at this infinite
second when their brown and green
was gold
For that moment when the
November sun found the perfect
angle and washed the trees of their
deep darkness with its waves of light
I felt the trees uproot and fly in this
moment
free of their future
buried in snow
torn by wind
free of all they have seen standing
in one place for decades
I swear I felt the hairs on the back of
their necks stand up as their very
existence was changed by this
insignificant break in cloud
I swear I heard them whisper

This went on forever and then was
over in a second
me and the trees laughing as we
sunbathed
me and the trees sighing as the
golden honey dripped and slid into
the moss at our feet

As the sun disappeared back into
the clouds, I swear I saw their boughs
tremble

My Forest of Unknown

—Kaitlyn Symons

Beginning this journey, I step into the forest of unknown
Their tall trunks are dark like prison bars
Liked together through their webbed structure
While unique and beautiful
They can hide and block the truth

The roots dig deep into the mud and soil
They tell the stories of struggles and triumphs
The thing is, the roots are hiding
Hiding any struggles from the rest of the world
Unable to seek help even if it is needed

The treetops catch the bright, yellow rays of sunshine
Rays of light and hope
They also catch the majority of dewy fresh rain
And endure the most through the dark storms

This forest has become part of me
Each part of the tree is going through something different
All making up the beautiful and ugly parts of what we call life
While at the beginning it was mostly unknown
The more you venture through the more you learn

Connecting the newfound knowledge to the world outside
We learn that everyone has their own forest of unknowns
Each proceeding at their own pace
Some may be near the treetops
While others closer to the roots
So take care of your forest and enjoy your journey through the unknown

Grow

—Toby Theriault

A child of the modern world
handed an axe
before his weak arms
could hold it high
Too young to comprehend
the wooden walls
which shelter him from wind and snow
Too young to see the fires
burning,
his forest of curiosity.
For him, the rings of a cedar are
infinite
eerie cut blocks and empty
mountainsides a horror yet to grace
his dreams
he sits oblivious and content on a
wooden chair.
To think, years from now, still a child
he will lie awake
those dreams tethered to his mind
no longer fantasies of sleep
but visible through open eyes
The eternal trees of his youth
seem to have become the elderly
even in their strength
their existence, fragile, delicate
The time of the Giants has come to
an end.
Leaving only children
to hark the trees' song of lament
yet he can cry no tears.
For a while he carries his axe of guilt
as a weapon
to sever the ugly head of greed
and seed the way of the future
Let those who come after
Grow.

ADULT

O McLellan Forest

—Susan McCaslin

(for the students of the Langley School of Fine Arts who came on Nov. 13, 2012, to make art for endangered McLellan Forest, Glen Valley, Langley, BC)

For the graced and gravitied trees
lolling by the Fraser, this green hymn

for green man, green woman, green child
mossed and tossed from green

for the unabashed tree huggers
who know it takes a village to save a forest

for Hopkins' Binsey Poplars
hacked and hewn

for the tall earth-honouring dream
and the dropping, dripping boughs

for the squadron of teens
streaming steadily from dirty yellow buses

into the sacred space to stand
among maidenhair ferns

with serenades for the mushroom stairway
climbing Cottonwood's hollowed heart

for the auric fairy rings still visible
to un-inventoried eyes

for the Councillors who would barter heritage
for a recreation centre elsewhere

deeper counsel, wisdom works
a pealed appeal rising

for all who long to be re-created
by mother world, held in green veils

chanting green

The forest named in the poem "O McLellan Forest," formerly known as "McLennan Forest East," was subsequently changed to The Blaauw Eco Forest. It is currently a nature reserve open to the public in Glen Valley east of Fort Langley, BC.

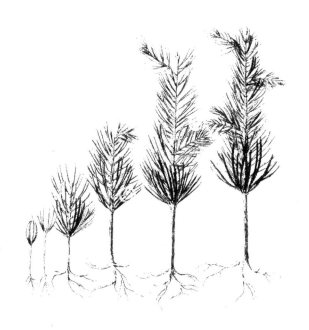

ABOUT THE EDITOR

PHOTO BY KATE CRAIG

Christine Lowther has been a lifelong activist and a resident of Clayoquot Sound since 1992. She is the author of three books of poetry, *New Power* (Broken Jaw Press, 1999), *My Nature* (Leaf Press, 2010), and *Half-Blood Poems* (Zossima Press, 2011). Her memoir, *Born Out of This* (Caitlin Press, 2014), was a finalist for the Roderick Haig-Brown Regional Prize at the 2015 BC Book Prizes. Christine is the editor of the poetry anthology *Worth More Standing: Poets and Activists Pay Homage to Trees* (Caitlin Press, 2022) and she co-edited two collections of essays, *Writing the West Coast: In Love with Place* (Ronsdale Press, 2008) and *Living Artfully: Reflections from the Far West Coast* (The Key Publishing House, 2012). Recipient of the inaugural Rainy Coast Arts Award for Significant Accomplishment in 2014, Chris served as Tofino Poet Laureate 2020-2022.

ABOUT THE CONTRIBUTORS

Aidan Zhang is from Vancouver, BC. He is a fast swimmer, skilled mountain biker and avid rower. He likes to read and he is a DIY tech nerd.

Aisha Hsu is from Burnaby, BC. She spends all her time doing Duolingo for German, playing video games, drawing and playing piano. Aisha also enjoys writing fiction or things about nature.

Alisa Wanyan is seven years old and she lives in West Vancouver, BC. She likes fencing and skating, and she works hard on them. She also likes giving her drawing to her friends and family as a present.

Alyssa Liu lives on the West Coast of BC. Her favourite activities include arts and crafts, swimming and gaming, and her favourite thing to do is hang out with all her friends.

Angela Wang is a student with many best friends at school. She is an artist and enjoys making bracelets and necklaces out of beads and playing with her toys.

Angelina Sunwoo lives in Vancouver, BC. Her life centres around art, including reading and painting. Much of her inspiration comes from nature, and the way it connects everyone and everything.

Angelina Xu likes to draw and do sports. She chose this tree as inspiration for her poem because she thought it was unique like every one of us. She sat under the tree with her notebook and started to write—she hopes you like her poem. Angelina lives in Vancouver, BC.

Annie Shen is a grade five student and the author of "Weeping Willow."

Anthony Li used to live in BC, Canada, but now lives in Sydney, Australia. His favourite activities include reading, reading and reading. His favourite things to read are books.

Bowen Wang is finishing high school at Magee Secondary School and hopes to study Marine Biology in the future at the university of Manao, Hawaii. Writing has allowed him to comprehend his own ideas. Writing for him always begins as a question.

Bronwyn Moes is from Vancouver Island. She loves to sing, paint and write in her free time. She also enjoys the outdoors which helped inspire her poem "The Tree Calls."

Carter Witter is a grade eight student from Ontario. He enjoys reading; playing chess; watching movies; studying math, religion & history, and playing video games.

Cedar Forest is a grade twelve student and the author of "I Swear I Saw Their Boughs Tremble."

Charley McLean is Métis and goes to the Environmental School in Maple Ridge. The inspiration for her poem came from knowing about the endangered old-growth trees in British Columbia.

Chester Trakarnsilpa is from Seattle. His favourite activities are football and baseball. In his free time he likes to play games and read books on his bed.

Chevy Trakarnsilpa is from Thailand. Chevy loves animals and that's why she wrote "Animals in Trees." Animals are unique—they come in all shapes, sizes and colours.

Doris Zhu is a grade two student and the author of "Me and My Maple Tree."

Emily Qian lives in Richmond, BC. She likes playing with her adorable puppy, Max, as well as writing poems and stories. Her love of nature often inspires her poems.

Ethan Wang is a grade five student and the author of "The Twisted Tree."

Harcus Yang lives on the coast of beautiful British Columbia. His favourite activities are hiking, skiing and reading books in his comfy chair under his fiddle tree.

Holly Zhang is a bubbly ten-year-old girl who loves the mountains and spending countless hours in the woods camping, biking, skiing and hiking. Holly hopes to become a veterinarian so she can help animals in the wild.

Isabel Wang is a grade four student from Delta, BC, and is the author of "The Cedar Tree."

Jet Robertson lives in Maple Ridge, BC. He loves to draw and be creative in many ways. He was inspired to write this poem while exploring in the forest one day.

Jon Manson is the author of "Native Mother."

Kaitlyn Symons lives in Victoria, BC. She wrote her poem with inspiration from walks through forests with her parents. Her favourite forest is Cathedral Grove in MacMillan Provincial Park.

Along with a spark of imagination, Kevin Wang leaves the reader in lasting thought through extraordinary visual description. He lives in Richmond, BC.

Krishti Khandelwal is a thirteen-year-old girl from Delhi, India. She loves to pen down her thoughts into words. During lockdown she created and shared her writing, and with the grace of God her writing got appreciated and encouraged by many.

Kristina Bedford is a student who loves volleyball, baking, reading and (of course) writing poetry. Her favourite activity is walking throughout her city with her father.

Lanice Chen loves to write essays and stories because it helps her imagine things and relax. In her spare time she watches TV and plays with her toys. Her favourite animal is the cat because it is fluffy and adorable.

Lucas Yu lives in West Vancouver, BC. He is a competitive ski racer, passionate runner, karate fighter, and swimmer. He loves playing the piano and solving math problems.

Luciana Lu lives in Vancouver, BC. Her favourite activities include playing basketball, swimming, skiing and playing piano. Her favorite things to plant are tulips and roses.

Lucy Yang is a BC teacher and writer. The found poem was collaboratively composed with hope by her grade eight students at Burnsview Secondary School in 2018–19.

Malia Ashby's poem was inspired by multiple amazing facts that create old growth trees, particularly the one undeniable fact that old growth trees are true survivors.

Matthew Ng lives in Vancouver, BC. His favourite activities are playing basketball, skiing, doing taekwondo, swimming, folding origami and playing video games.

Maya Mior is a young poet living near Vancouver, BC. Her favourite activities include biking, unicycling, and swimming, and she loves collecting houseplants of all shapes and sizes.

Noelle Fung resides in a modest accommodation, encased by garden greenery where couples take their wedding pictures. She hates plants and is scared of toasters, yet she has both.

Oafe Cheung lives in Vancouver, BC. Some things she likes to do in her free time are reading books and playing the piano.

Ocea Green lives in Tofino, BC. She loves to surf, do art, surf again and be in nature. She is always up for an adventure.

Paul Phillos lives on the North-West Coast of BC. Some of his favourite things to do include going on hikes with his family, reading books and playing videogames with friends.

Riley Tam lives in Vancouver, BC. He enjoys listening to melodic rap and creating computer art. His favourite activity is to play basketball with his friends and team.

Rio Green is a keen birder and loves nature, animals and trees. She likes to write stories and funny jokey comics about animals. She lives in Tofino, BC.

Roselyn Tam lives in Vancouver, BC. She enjoys listening and dancing to K-pop music. In her spare time, her favourite activities include drawing, making jewelry and dancing.

Ryan Kossari lives in Vancouver, BC. One day Ryan was in Whistler eating fish tacos when a poem sparked his mind. He spends his extra time writing and taking pictures of nature.

Ryder Hsu is from Burnaby, BC. He spends time playing piano, chess, and videogames, and also likes to jump on his trampoline. Ryder also enjoys cooking with his family members.

Sophia (Saifeier) Zhang loves writing because she feels writing can help her to express observations about feelings and nature. Writing offers a way of sharing her thoughts with the world.

Saioa Ouyoumjian is an avid reader and hopes to be an author someday. She enjoys playing violin, rock climbing, skiing, watching movies with her family and snuggling with her dog, Lolo.

Vancouver-born, eleven-year-old Samantha Pon enjoys figure skating, reading, and adoring cup poodles. The author of "Sakuras" chose cherry blossom trees because of the breathtaking beauty of the flowers.

Sofia Varma-Vitug is a fourteen-year-old writer, athlete and avid reader. She loves writing poetry and fiction. To Sofia, writing is a way to find and make beauty in the world.

Soleil Zhang loves to fence and to read the Ranger's Apprentice series. She is writing a fiction book. She likes writing because it lets her take a break from subjects like math.

Susan McCaslin is a Canadian poet residing in Fort Langley, BC, who has published sixteen volumes of poetry, including *Into the Open: Poems New and Selected* (Inanna, 2017). Susan's early chapbook, *Letters to William Blake*, was the first-place winner of the Mother Tongue Chapbook Competition for 1997, adjudicated by P.K. Page. It was produced on a handset press by Mona Fertig and Peter Haase of Mother Tongue Publishing (Salt Spring Island, BC). Susan initiated the Han Shan Poetry Project in 2012, which helped save an endangered forest in Glen Valley near her home. www.susanmccaslin.ca

Sylvester Gross-Hamburger is a Seattle poet and brother to two amazing sisters. Currently, he is indulging himself in a resurgence of his elementary school Monster High phase.

Tanis Cortens loves reading, writing, drinking tea and going for walks in nature. Her favourite place to hike is Westwood Lake Park in Nanaimo, BC.

Toby Theriault is a grade twelve student and the author of "Grow."

Ty Joudrey grew up on Gabriola Island and in Ucluelet, BC. He always misses the arbutus trees, as they do not grow on the west side of the Island.

Warren Liu is a grade one student and the author of "Warren's Tree."

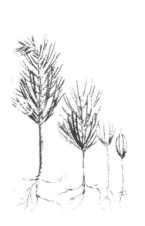